AN IRON WILL

ORISON SWETT MARDEN

CONTENTS

Chapter

AN IRON WILL

Chapter I. Trainning The Will

"The education of the will is the object of our existence,"
says Emerson.

N or is this putting it too strongly, if we take into account the human will in its relations to the divine. This accords with the saying of J. Stuart Mill, that "a character is a completely fashioned will."In respect to mere mundane relations, the development and discipline of one's will-power is of supreme moment in relation to success in life. No man can ever estimate the power of will. It is a part of the divine nature, all of a piece with the power of creation. We speak of God's fiat "_Fiat lux_, Let light be." Man has his fiat. The achievements of history have been the choices, the determinations, the creations, of the human will. It was the will, quiet or pugnacious, gentle or grim, of men like Wilberforce and Garrison, Goodyear and Cyrus Field, Bismarck and Grant, that made them indomitable. They simply would do what they planned. Such men can no more be stopped than the sun can be, or the tide. Most men fail, not through lack of education or agreeable personal qualities, but from lack of dogged determination, from lack of dauntless will.

"It is impossible," says Sharman, "to look into the conditions under which the battle of life is being fought, without perceiving how much really depends upon the extent to which the will-power is cultivated, strengthened, and made operative in right directions." Young people need to go into training for it. We live in an age of athletic meets. Those who are determined to have athletic will-power must take for it the kind of exercise they need.

This is well illustrated by a report I have seen of the long race from Marathon in the recent Olympian games, which was won by the young Greek peasant, Sotirios Loues.

A STRUGGLE IN THE RACE OF LIFE.

There had been no great parade about the training of this champion runner. From his work at the plough he quietly betook himself to the task of making Greece victorious before the assembled strangers from every land. He was known to be a good runner, and without fuss or bustle he entered himself as a competitor. But it was not his speed alone, out-distancing every rival, that made the young Greek stand out from among his fellows that day. When he left his cottage home at Amarusi, his father said to him, "Sotiri, you must only return a victor!" The light of a firm resolve shone in the young man's eye. The old father was sure that his boy would win, and so he made his way to the station, there to wait till Sotiri should come in ahead of all the rest. No one knew the old man and his three daughters as they elbowed their way through the crowd. When at last the excitement of the assembled multitude told that the critical moment had arrived, that the racers were nearing the goal, the old father looked up through eyes that were a little dim as he realized that truly Sotiri was leading the way. He _was_ "returning a victor." How the crowd surged about the young peasant when the race was fairly won! Wild with excitement, they knew not how to shower upon him sufficient praise. Ladies overwhelmed him with flowers and rings; some even gave him their watches, and one American lady bestowed upon him her jewelled smelling-bottle. The princes embraced him, and the king himself saluted him in military fashion. But the young Sotirios was seeking for other praise than theirs. Past the ranks of royalty and fair maidenhood, past the outstretched hands of his own countrymen, past the applauding crowd of foreigners, his gaze wandered till it fell upon an old man trembling with eagerness, who resolutely pushed his way through the excited, satisfied throng. Then the young face lighted, and as old Loues advanced to the innermost circle with arms outstretched to embrace his boy, the young victor said, simply: "You see, father, I have obeyed."

MENTAL DISCIPLINE.

The athlete trains for his race; and the mind must be put into training if one will win life's race.

"It is," says Professor Mathews, "only by continued, strenuous efforts, repeated again and again, day after day, week after week, and month after month, that the ability can be acquired to fasten the mind to one subject, however abstract or knotty, to the exclusion of everything else. The process of obtaining this self-mastery--this complete command of one's mental powers--is a gradual one, its length varying with the mental constitution of each person; but its acquisition is worth infinitely more than the utmost labor it ever costs."

"Perhaps the most valuable result of all education," it was said by Professor Huxley, "is the ability to make yourself do the thing you have to do when it ought to be done, whether you like it or not; it is the first lesson which ought to be learned, and, however early a man's training begins, it is probably the last lesson which he learns thoroughly."

DOING THINGS ONCE.

When Henry Ward Beecher was asked how it was that he could accomplish so much more than other men, he replied: "I don't do more, but less, than other people. They do all their work three times over: once in anticipation, once in actuality, once in rumination. I do mine in actuality alone, doing it once instead of three times."

This was by the intelligent exercise of Mr. Beecher's will-power in concentrating his mind upon what he was doing at a given moment, and then turning to something else. Any one who has observed business men closely, has noticed this characteristic. One of the secrets of a successful life is to be able to hold all of our energies upon one point, to focus all of the scattered rays of the mind upon one place or thing.

CENTRALIZING FORCE.

The mental reservoir of most people is like a leaky dam which we sometimes see in the country, where the greater part of the water flows out without going over the wheel and doing the work of the mill. The habit of mind-wandering, of worrying about this and that,

"Genius, that power which dazzles mortal eyes,   Is oft but Perseverance in disguise."

Many a man would have been a success had he connected his fragmentary efforts. Spasmodic, disconnected attempts, without concentration, uncontrolled by any fixed idea, will never bring success. It is continuity of purpose alone that achieves results.

LEARNING TO SWIM.

The way to learn to run is to run, the way to learn to swim is to swim. The way to learn to develop will-power is by the actual exercise of will-power in the business of life. "The man that exercises his will," says an English essayist, "makes it a stronger and more effective force in proportion to the extent to which such exercise is intelligently and perseveringly maintained." The forth-putting of will-power is a means of strengthening will-power. The will becomes strong by exercise. To stick to a thing till you are master, is a test of intellectual discipline and power.

DR. CUYLER.

"It is astonishing," says Dr. Theodore Cuyler, "how many men lack this power of 'holding on' until they reach the goal. They can make a sudden dash, but they lack grit. They are easily discouraged. They get on as long as everything goes smoothly, but when there is friction they lose heart. They depend on stronger personalities for their spirit and strength. They lack independence or originality. They only dare to do what others do. They do not step boldly from the crowd and act fearlessly."

THE BIG TREES.

What is needed by him who would succeed in the highest degree possible is careful planning. He is to accumulate reserved power, that he may be equal to all emergencies. Thomas Starr King said that the great trees of California gave him his first impression of the power of reserve. "It was the thought of the reserve energies that had been compacted into them," he said, "that stirred me.

The mountains had given them their iron and rich stimulants, the hills had given them their soil, the clouds had given their rain and snow, and a thousand summers and winters had poured forth their treasures about their vast roots."

No young man can hope to do anything above the commonplace who has not made his life a reservoir of power on which he can constantly draw, which will never fail him in any emergency. Be sure that you have stored away, in your power-house, the energy, the knowledge that will be equal to the great occasion when it comes. "If I were twenty, and had but ten years to live," said a great scholar and writer, "I would spend the first nine years accumulating knowledge and getting ready for the tenth."

"I WILL."

"There are no two words in the English language which stand out in bolder relief, like kings upon a checker-board, to so great an extent as the words 'I will.' There is strength, depth and solidity, decision, confidence and power, determination, vigor and individuality, in the round, ringing tone which characterizes its delivery. It talks to you of triumph over difficulties, of victory in the face of discouragement, of will to promise and strength to perform, of lofty and daring enterprise, of unfettered aspirations, and of the thousand and one solid impulses by which man masters impediments in the way of progression."

As one has well said: "He who is silent is forgotten; he who does not advance falls back; he who stops is overwhelmed, distanced, crushed; he who ceases to become greater, becomes smaller; he who leaves off gives up; the stationary is the beginning of the end--it precedes death; to live is to achieve, to will without ceasing."

*"Be thou a hero; let thy might
ramp on eternal snows its way,
And through the ebon walls of night,
Hew down a passage unto day."*

--Park Benjamin

Chapter II. The Rulers Of Destiny.

There is no chance, no destiny, no fate,
Can circumvent, or hinder, or control
The firm resolve of a determined soul.
Gifts count for nothing; will alone is great;
All things give way before it soon or late.
What obstacle can stay the mighty force
Of the sea-seeking river in its course,
Or cause the ascending orb of day to wait?
Each well-born soul must win what it deserves.
Let the fool prate of luck. The fortunate
Is he whose earnest purpose never swerves,
Whose slightest action or inaction serves
The one great aim.

--Ella Wheeler Wilcox

There is always room for a man of force.--Emerson.
The king is the man who can.--Carlyle.
A strong, defiant purpose is many-handed, and lays hold of whatever is near that can serve it; it has a magnetic power that draws to itself whatever is kindred.--T.T. Munger.

What is will-power, looked at in a large way, but energy of character? Energy of will, self-originating force, is the soul of every great character. Where it is, there is life; where it is not, there is faintness, helplessness, and despondency. "Let it be your first study to teach the world that you are not wood and straw; that there is some iron in you." Men who have left their mark upon the world have been men of great and prompt decision. The achievements of will-power are almost beyond computation. Scarcely anything seems impossible to the man who can will strongly enough and long enough. One talent with a will behind it will accomplish more than ten without it, as a thimbleful of powder in a rifle, the bore of whose barrel will give it direction, will do greater execution than a carload burned in the open air.

"THE WILLS, THE WON'TS, AND THE CAN'TS."

"There are three kinds of people in the world," says a recent writer, "the wills, the won'ts, and the can'ts. The first accomplish everything; the second oppose everything; the third fail in every-thing."

The shores of fortune, as Foster says, are covered with the stranded wrecks of men of brilliant ability, but who have wanted courage, faith, and decision, and have therefore perished in sight of more resolute but less capable adventurers, who succeeded in mak-ing port.

Were I called upon to express in a word the secret of so many failures among those who started out with high hopes, I should say they lacked will-power. They could not half will: and what is a man without a will? He is like an engine without steam. Genius unexecuted is no more genius than a bushel of acorns is a forest of oaks.

Will has been called the spinal column of personality. "The will in its relation to life," says an English writer, "may be compared at once to the rudder and to the steam engine of a vessel, on the confined and related action of which it depends entirely for the direction of its course and the vigor of its movement."

Strength of will is the test of a young man's possibilities. Can he will strong enough, and hold whatever he undertakes with an iron grip? It is the iron grip that takes and holds. What chance is there in this crowding, pushing, selfish, greedy world, where everything is pusher or pushed, for a young man with no will, no grip on life? The man who would forge to the front in this competitive age must be a man of prompt and determined decision.

A TAILOR'S NEEDLE.

It is in one of Ben Jonson's old plays: "When I once take the humor of a thing, I am like your tailor's needle--I go through with it."

This is not different from Richelieu, who said: "When I have once taken a resolution, I go straight to my aim; I overthrow all, I cut down all."

And in business affairs the counsel of Rothschild is to the same effect: "Do without fail that which you determine to do."

Gladstone's children were taught to accomplish _to the end_ whatever they might begin, no matter how insignificant the undertaking might be.

WHAT IS WORSE THAN RASHNESS

It is irresolution that is worse than rashness. "He that shoots," says Feltham, "may sometimes hit the mark; but he that shoots not at all can never hit it. Irresolution is like an ague; it shakes not this nor that limb, but all the body is at once in a fit."

The man who is forever twisting and turning, backing and

filling, hesitating and dawdling, shuffling and parleying, weighing and balancing, splitting hairs over non-essentials, listening to every new motive which presents itself, will never accomplish anything. But the positive man, the decided man, is a power in the world, and stands for something; you can measure him, and estimate the work that his energy will accomplish.

Opportunity is coy, is swift, is gone, before the slow, the unobservant, the indolent, or the careless can seize her. "Vigilance in watching opportunity," said Phelps, "tact and daring in seizing upon opportunity; force and persistence in crowding opportunity to its utmost of possible achievement--these are the martial virtues which must command success." "The best men," remarked Chapin, "are not those who have waited for chances, but who have taken them; besieged the chance; conquered the chance; and made chance the servitor."

Is it not possible to classify successes and failures by their various degrees of will-power? A man who can resolve vigorously upon a course of action, and turns neither to the right nor to the left, though a paradise tempt him, who keeps his eyes upon the goal, whatever distracts him, is sure of success.

"Not every vessel that sails from Tarshish will bring back the gold of Ophir. But shall it therefore rot in the harbor? No! Give its sails to the wind!"

CONSCIOUS POWER.

"Conscious power," says Melles, "exists within the mind of every one. Sometimes its existence is unrealized, but it is there. It is there to be developed and brought forth, like the culture of that obstinate but beautiful flower, the orchid. To allow it to remain dormant is to place one's self in obscurity, to trample on one's ambition, to smother one's faculties. To develop it is to individualize all that is best within you, and give it to the world. It is by an absolute knowledge of yourself, the proper estimate of your own value."

"There is hardly a reader," says an experienced educator, "who will not be able to recall the early life of at least one young man whose childhood was spent in poverty, and who, in boyhood, expressed a firm desire to secure a higher education. If, a little later, that desire became a declared resolve, soon the avenues opened to that end. That desire and resolve created an atmosphere which attracted the forces necessary to the attainment of the purpose. Many of these young men will tell us that, as long as they were hoping and striving and longing, mountains of difficulty rose before them; but that when they fashioned their hopes into fixed purposes aid came unsought to help them on the way."

DO YOU BELIEVE IN YOURSELF?

The man without self-reliance and an iron will is the plaything of chance, the puppet of his environment, the slave of circumstances. Are not doubts the greatest of enemies? If you would succeed up to the limit of your possibilities, must you not constantly hold to the belief that you are success-organized, and that you will be successful, no matter what opposes? You are never to allow a shadow of doubt to enter your mind that the Creator intended you to win in life's battle. Regard every suggestion that your life may be a failure, that you are not made like those who succeed, and that success is not for you, as a traitor, and expel it from your mind as you would a thief from your house.

There is something sublime in the youth who possesses the spirit of boldness and fearlessness, who has proper confidence in his ability to do and dare.

The world takes us at our own valuation. It believes in the man who believes in himself, but it has little use for the timid man, the one who is never certain of himself; who cannot rely on his own judgment, who craves advice from others, and is afraid to go ahead on his own account.

It is the man with a positive nature, the man who believes that he is equal to the emergency, who believes he can do the thing he attempts, who wins the confidence of his fellow-man. He is beloved because he is brave and self-sufficient.

Those who have accomplished great things in the world have been, as a rule, bold, aggressive, and self-confident. They dared to step out from the crowd, and act in an original way. They were not afraid to be generals.

There is little room in this crowding, competing age for the timid, vacillating youth. He who would succeed to-day must not only be brave, but must also dare to take chances. He who waits for certainty never wins.

"The law of the soul is eternal endeavor,   That bears the man onward and upward forever."

"A man can be too confiding in others, but never too confident in himself."

Never admit defeat or poverty. Stoutly assert your divine right to hold your head up and look the world in the face; step bravely to the front whatever opposes, and the world will make way for you. No one will insist upon your rights while you yourself doubt that you have any. Believe you were made for the place you fill. Put forth your whole energies. Be awake, electrify yourself; go forth to the task. A young man once said to his employer, "Don't give me an easy job. I want to handle heavy boxes, shoulder great loads. I would like to lift a big mountain and throw it into the sea,"--and he stretched out two brawny arms, while his honest eyes danced and his whole being glowed with conscious strength.

The world in its heart admires the stern, determined doer. "The world turns aside to let any man pass who knows whither he is going." "It is wonderful how even the apparent casualties of life seem to bow to a spirit that will not bow to them, and yield to assist a design, after having in vain attempted to frustrate it."

"The man who succeeds," says Prentice Mulford, "must always in mind or imagination live, move, think, and act as if he gained that success, or he never will gain it."

"We go forth," said Emerson, "austere, dedicated, believing in the iron links of Destiny, and will not turn on our heels to save our lives. A book, a bust, or only the sound of a name shoots a spark through the nerves, and we suddenly believe in will. We cannot hear of personal vigor of any kind, great power of performance, without fresh resolution."

Chapter III. Force of Will In Camp And Field

Oh, what miracles have been wrought by the self-confidence, the self-determination of an iron will! What impossible deeds have been performed by it! It was this that took Napoleon over the Alps in midwinter; it took Farragut and Dewey past the cannons, torpedoes, and mines of the enemy; it led Nelson and Grant to victory; it has been the great tonic in the world of discovery, invention, and art; it has helped to win the thousand triumphs in war and science which were deemed impossible.

The secret of Jeanne d'Arc's success was not alone in rare decision of character, but in the seeing of visions which inspired her to self-confidence--confidence in her divine mission.
It was an iron will that gave Nelson command of the British fleet, a title, and a statue at Trafalgar Square It was the keynote of his character when he said, "When I don't know whether to fight or not, I always fight."

It was an iron will that was brought into play when Horatius with two companions held ninety thousand Tuscans at bay until the bridge across the Tiber had been destroyed--when Leonidas at Thermopylae checked the mighty march of Xerxes--when Themistocles off the coast of Greece shattered the Persian's Armada--when Caesar finding his army hard pressed seized spear and buckler and snatched victory from defeat--when Winkelried gathered to his breast a sheaf of Austrian spears and opened a path for his comrades--when Wellington fought in many climes without ever being conquered--when Ney on a hundred fields changed apparent disaster into brilliant triumph--when Sheridan arrived from Winchester as the Union retreat was becoming a route and turned the tide--when Sherman signaled his men to hold the fort knowing that their leader was coming.

History furnishes thousands of examples of men who have seized occasions to accomplish results deemed impossible by those less resolute. Prompt decision and whole-souled action sweep the world before them. Who was the organizer of the modern German empire? Was he not the man of iron?

NAPOLEON AND GRANT.

"What would you do if you were besieged in a place entirely destitute of provisions?" asked the examiner, when Napoleon was a cadet.

"If there were anything to eat in the enemy's camp, I should not be concerned."

When Paris was in the hands of a mob, and the authorities were panic-stricken, in came a man who said, "I know a young officer who can quell this mob."

"Send for him."

Napoleon was sent for; he came, he subjugated the mob, he subjugated the authorities, he ruled France, then conquered Europe.

May 10, 1796, Napoleon carried the bridge at Lodi, in the face of the Austrian batteries, trained upon the French end of the structure. Behind them were six thousand troops. Napoleon massed four thousand grenadiers at the head of the bridge, with a battalion of three hundred carbineers in front. At the tap of the drum the foremost assailants wheeled from the cover of the street wall under a terrible hail of grape and canister, and attempted to pass the gateway to the bridge. The front ranks went down like stalks of grain before a reaper; the column staggered and reeled backward, and the valiant grenadiers were appalled by the task before them. Without a word or a look of reproach Napoleon placed himself at their head, and his aids and generals rushed to his side. Forward again over heaps of dead that choked the passage, and a quick run counted by seconds only carried the column across two hundred yards of clear space, scarcely a shot from the Austrians taking effect beyond the point where the platoons wheeled for the first leap. _The guns of the enemy were not aimed at the advance. The advance was too quick for the Austrian gunners_. So sudden and so miraculous was it all, that the Austrian artillerists abandoned their guns instantly, and their supports fled in a panic instead of rushing to the front and meeting the French onslaught. This Napoleon had counted on in making the bold attack.

What was Napoleon but the thunderbolt of war? He once journeyed from Spain to Paris at seventeen miles an hour in the saddle.

"Is it _possible_ to cross the path?" asked Napoleon of the engineers who had been sent to explore the dreaded pass of St. Bernard.

"Perhaps," was the hesitating reply, "it is within the limits of _possibility_."

"*Forward, then.*"

Yet Ulysses S. Grant, a young man unknown to fame, with neither money nor influence, with no patrons or friends, in six years fought more battles, gained more victories, captured more prisoners, took more spoils, commanded more men, than Napoleon did in twenty years. "The great thing about him," said Lincoln, "is cool persistence."

"DON'T SWEAR--FIGHT."

When the Spanish fire on San Juan Hill became almost unbearable, some of the Rough Riders began to swear. Colonel Wood, with the wisdom of a good leader, called out, amid the whistle of the Mauser bullets: "Don't swear--fight!"

In a skirmish at Salamanca, while the enemy's guns were pouring shot into his regiment, Sir William Napier's men became disobedient. He at once ordered a halt, and flogged four of the ringleaders under fire. The men yielded at once, and then marched three miles under a heavy cannonade as coolly as if it were a review.

When Pellisier, the Crimean chief of Zouaves, struck an officer with a whip, the man drew a pistol that missed fire. The chief replied: "Fellow, I order you a three days' arrest for not having your arms in better order."

The man of iron will is cool in the hour of danger.

"I HAD TO RUN LIKE A CYCLONE."

This was what Roosevelt said about his pushing on up San Juan Hill ahead of his regiment: "I had to run like a cyclone to stay in front and keep from being run over."

The personal heroism of Hobson, or of Cushing, who blew up the "Albemarle" forty years ago, was but the expression of a magnificent will power. It was this which was the basis of General Wheeler's unparalleled military advancement: a second lieutenant at twenty-three, a colonel at twenty-four, a brigadier-general at twenty-five, a major-general at twenty-six, a corps commander at twenty-seven, and a lieutenant-general at twenty-eight.

General Wheeler had sixteen horses killed under him, and a great number wounded. His saddle equipments and clothes were frequently struck by the missiles of the enemy. He was three times wounded, once painfully. He had thirty-two staff officers, or acting staff officers, killed or wounded. In almost every case they were immediately by his side. No officer was ever more exposed to the missiles of death than Joseph Wheeler.

What is this imperial characteristic of manhood, an iron will, but that which underlies all magnificent achievement, whether by heroes of the "Light Brigade" or the heroic fire-fighters of our great cities?

Chapter IV. Will Power In Its Relation To Health And Disease

I.

THERE is no doubt that, as a rule, great decision of character is usually accompanied by great constitutional firmness. Men who have been noted for great firmness of character have usually been strong and robust. As a rule it is the strong physical man who carries weight and conviction. Take, as an example, William the Conqueror, as he is pictured by Green in his history:

"The very spirit of the sea-robbers from whom he sprang seemed embodied in his gigantic form, his enormous strength, his savage countenance, his desperate bravery. No other knight under heaven, his enemies confessed, was William's peer. No other man could bend William's bow. His mace crashed through a ring of English warriors to the foot of the standard. He rose to his greatest heights in moments when other men despaired. No other man who ever sat upon the throne of England was this man's match."

Or, take Webster. Sydney Smith said: "Webster is a living lie; because no man on earth can be as great as he looks." Carlyle said of him: "One would incline at sight to back him against the world." His very physique was eloquent. Men yielded their wills to his at sight.

The great prizes of life ever fall to the robust, the stalwart, the strong,--not to a huge muscle or powerful frame necessarily, but to a strong vitality, a great nervous energy. It is the Lord Broughams, working almost continuously one hundred and forty-four hours; it is the Napoleons, twenty hours in the saddle; it is the Franklins, camping out in the open air at seventy; it is the Gladstones, firmly grasping the helm of the ship of state at eighty-four, tramping miles every day, and chopping down huge trees at eighty-five,--who accomplish the great things of life.

To prosper you must improve your brain power; and nothing helps the brain more than a healthy body. The race of to-day is only to be won by those who will study to keep their bodies in such good condition that their minds are able and ready to sustain that high pressure on memory and mind, which our present fierce competition engenders. It is health rather than strength that is now wanted. Health is essentially the requirement of our time to enable us to succeed in life. In all modern occupations--from the nursery to the school, from the school to the shop or world beyond--the brain and nerve strain go on, continuous, augmenting, and intensifying.

As a rule physical vigor is the condition of a great career. Stonewall Jackson, early in life, determined to conquer every weakness he had, physical, mental, and moral. He held all of his powers with a firm hand. To his great self-discipline and self-mastery he owed his success. So determined was he to harden himself to the weather that he could not be induced to wear an overcoat in winter. "I will not give in to the cold," he said. For a year, on account of dyspepsia, he lived on buttermilk and stale bread, and wore a wet shirt next his body because his doctor advised it, although everybody else ridiculed the idea. This was while he was professor at the Virginia Military Institute. His doctor advised him to retire at nine o'clock; and, no matter where he was, or who was present, he always sought his bed on the minute. He adhered rigidly through life to this stern system of discipline. Such self-training, such self-conquest, gives one great power over others. It is equal to genius itself.

"I can do nothing," said Grant, "without nine hours' sleep."

What else is so grand as to stand on life's threshold, fresh, young, hopeful, with a consciousness of power equal to any emergency,--a master of the situation? The glory of a young man is his strength.

Our great need of the world to-day is for men and women who are good animals. To endure the strain of our concentrated civilization, the coming man and woman must have an excess of animal spirits. They must have a robustness of health. Mere absence of disease is not health. It is the overflowing fountain, not the one half full, that gives life and beauty to the valley below. Only he is healthy who exults in mere animal existence; whose very life is a luxury; who feels a bounding pulse throughout his body; who feels life in every limb, as dogs do when scouring over the field, or as boys do when gliding over fields of ice.

II.

Yet in spite of all this, in defiance of it, we know that an iron will is often triumphant in the contest with physical infirmity.

"Brave spirits are a balsam to themselves: There is a nobleness of mind that heals   Wounds beyond salves."

"One day," said a noted rope-walker, "I signed an agreement to wheel a barrow along a rope on a given day. A day or two before I was seized with lumbago. I called in my medical man, and told him I must be cured by a certain day; not only because I should lose what I hoped to earn, but also forfeit a large sum. I got no better, and the doctor forbade my getting up. I told him, 'What do I want with your advice? If you cannot cure me, of what good is your advice?' When I got to the place, there was the doctor protesting I was unfit for the exploit. I went on, though I felt like a frog with my back. I got ready my pole and my barrow, took hold of the handles and wheeled it along the rope as well as I ever did. When I got to the end I wheeled it back again, and when this was done I was a frog again. What made me that I could wheel the barrow? It was my reserve will."

"What does he know," asks the sage, "who has not suffered?" Did not Schiller produce his greatest tragedies in the midst of physical suffering almost amounting to torture? Handel was never greater than when, warned by palsy of the approach of death, and struggling with distress and suffering, he sat down to compose the great works which have made his name immortal in music. Beethoven was almost totally deaf and burdened with sorrow when he produced his greatest works. Milton writing "Who best can suffer, best can do," wrote at his best when in feeble health, and when poor and blind.

"...Yet I argue not   Against Heaven's hand or will, nor bate a jot Of heart or hope; but still bear up and steer   Right onward."
The Rev. William H. Milburn, who lost his sight when a child, studied for the ministry, and was ordained before he attained his majority. He has written half a dozen books, among them a very careful history of the Mississippi Valley. He has long been chaplain of the lower house of Congress.

Blind Fanny Crosby, of New York, was a teacher of the blind for many years. She has written nearly three thousand hymns, among which are: "Pass Me not, O Gentle Saviour," "Rescue the Perishing," "Saviour More than Life to Me," and "Jesus keep Me near the Cross."

"The truest help we can render one who is afflicted," said Bishop Brooks, "is not to take his burden from him, but to call out his best energy, that he may be able to bear."

What a mighty will Darwin had! He was in continual ill health. He was in constant suffering. His patience was marvellous. No one but his wife knew what he endured. "For forty years," says his son, "he never knew one day of health;" yet during those forty years he unremittingly forced himself to do the work from which the mightiest minds and the strongest constitutions would have shrunk. He had a wonderful power of sticking to a subject. He used almost to apologize for his patience, saying that he could not bear to be beaten, as if it were a sign of weakness.

Bulwer advises us to refuse to be ill, never to tell people we are ill, never to own it ourselves. Illness is one of those things which a man should resist on principle. Do not dwell upon your ailments nor study your symptoms. Never allow yourself to be convinced that you are not complete master of yourself. Stoutly affirm your own superiority over bodily ills. We should keep a high ideal of health and harmony constantly before the mind.

Is not the mind the natural protector of the body? We cannot believe that the Creator has left the whole human race entirely at the mercy of only about half a dozen specific drugs which always act with certainty. There is a divine remedy placed within us for many of the ills we suffer. If we only knew how to use this power of will and mind to protect ourselves, many of us would be able to carry youth and cheerfulness with us into the teens of our second century. The mind has undoubted power to preserve and sustain physical youth and beauty, to keep the body strong and healthy, to renew life, and to preserve it from decay, many years longer than it does now. The longest-lived men and women have, as a rule, been those who have attained great mental and moral development. They have lived in the upper region of a higher life, beyond the reach of much of the jar, the friction, and the discords which weaken and shatter most lives. Every physician knows that courageous people, with indomitable will, are not half as likely to contract contagious diseases as the timid, the vacillating, the irresolute. A thoughtful physician once assured a friend that if an express agent were to visit New Orleans in the yellow-fever season, having forty thousand dollars in his care, he would be in little danger of the fever so long as he kept possession of the money. Let him once deliver that into other hands, and the sooner he left the city the better.

Napoleon used to visit the plague hospitals even when the physicians dreaded to go, and actually put his hands upon the plague-stricken patients. He said the man who was not afraid could vanish the plague. A will power like this is a strong tonic to the body. Such a will has taken many men from apparent death-beds, and enabled them to perform wonderful deeds of valor. When told by his physicians that he must die, Douglas Jerrold said: "And leave a family of helpless children? I won't die." He kept his word, and lived for years.

Chapter V. The Romance of Achievement Under Difficulties

"What doth the poor man's son inherit?
Stout muscles, and a sinewy heart,
A hardy frame, a hardier spirit!
King of two hands he does his partn
In every useful toil and art:
A heritage it seems to me,
A king might wish to hold in fee."

--Lowell

HAS not God given every man a capital to start with? Are we not born rich? He is rich who has good health, a sound body, good muscles; he is rich who has a good head, a good disposition, a good heart; he is rich who has two good hands, with five chances on each. Equipped? Every man is equipped as only God could equip him. What a fortune he possesses in the marvellous mechanism of his body and mind. It is individual effort that has achieved everything worth achieving.

THE FUN OF THE LITTLE GAME.

A big Australian, six feet four, James Tyson, died not long since, with a property of $25,000,000, who began life as a farm hand. Tyson cared little for money. He used to say of it:

"I shall just leave it behind me when I go. I shall have done with it then, and it will not concern me afterwards. But," he would add, with a characteristic semi-exultant snap of the fingers, "the money is nothing. It was the little game that was the fun."

Being asked, "What was the little game?" he replied with an energy of concentration peculiar to him: "_Fighting the desert_. That has been my work. I have been fighting the desert all my life, and I have won. I have put water where was no water, and beef where was no beef. I have put fences where there were no fences, and roads where there were no roads. Nothing can undo what I have done, and millions will be happier for it after I am long dead and forgotten."

Has not self-help accomplished about all the great things of the world? How many young men falter, faint, and dally with their purpose because they have no capital to start with, and wait and wait for some good luck to give them a lift. But success is the child of drudgery and perseverance. It cannot be coaxed or bribed; pay the price, and it is yours. A constant struggle, a ceaseless battle to bring success from inhospitable surroundings, is the price of all great achievements.

CONQUERORS OF FORTUNE.

Benjamin Franklin had this tenacity of purpose in a wonderful degree. When he started in the printing business in Philadelphia, he carried his material through the streets on a wheelbarrow. He hired one room for his office, work-room, and sleeping-room. He found a formidable rival in the city and invited him to his room. Pointing to a piece of bread from which he had just eaten his dinner, he said:

"Unless you can live cheaper than I can, you cannot starve me out."

It was so that he proved the wisdom of Edmund Burke's saying, that "He that wrestles with us strengthens our nerves, and sharpens our skill: our antagonist is our helper."

The poor and friendless lad, George Peabody, weary, foot-sore, and hungry, called at a tavern in Concord, N.H., and asked to be allowed to saw wood for lodging and breakfast. Yet he put in work for everything he ever received, and out-matched the poverty of early days.

Gideon Lee could not even get shoes to wear in winter, when a boy, but he went to work barefoot in the snow. He made a bargain with himself to work sixteen hours a day. He fulfilled it to the letter, and when from interruption he lost time, he robbed himself of sleep to make it up. He became a wealthy merchant of New York, mayor of the city, and a member of Congress.

COMMERCIAL COURAGE.

The business affairs of a gentleman named Rouss were once in a complicated condition, owing to his conflicting interests in various states, and he was thrown into prison. While confined he wrote on the walls of his cell:

"I am forty years of age this day. When I am fifty, I shall be worth half a million; and by the time I am sixty, I shall be worth a million dollars."

He lived to accumulate more than three million dollars.

"The ruin which overtakes so many merchants," says Whipple, "is due not so much to their lack of business talent as to their lack of business nerve."

Cyrus W. Field had retired from business with a large fortune when he became possessed with the idea that by means of a cable laid upon the bottom of the Atlantic Ocean, telegraphic communication could be established between Europe and America. He plunged into the undertaking with all the force of his being. It was an incredibly hard contest: the forests of Newfoundland, the lobby in Congress, the unskilled handling of brakes on his Agamemnon cable, a second and a third breaking of the cable at sea, the cessation of the current in a well-laid cable, the snapping of a superior cable on the Great Eastern--all these availed not to foil the iron will of Field, whose final triumph was that of mental energy in the application of science.

FOUR NEW YORK JOURNALISTS.

To Horace Greeley, the founder of the "Tribune," I need not a lude; his story is or ought to be in every school-book. James Brooks, once the editor and proprietor of the "Daily Express," and later an eminent congressman, began life as a clerk in a store in Maine, and when twenty-one received for his pay a hogshead of New England rum. He was so eager to go to college that he started for Waterville with his trunk on his back, and when he was graduated he was so poor and plucky that he carried his trunk on his back to the station as he went home.

When James Gordon Bennett was forty years old he collected all his property, three hundred dollars, and in a cellar with a board upon two barrels for a desk, himself his own typesetter, office boy, publisher, newsboy, clerk, editor, proofreader, and printer's devil, he started the "New York Herald." He did this, after many attempts and defeats in trying to follow the routine, instead of doing his own way. Never was any man's early career a better illustration of Wendell Phillips' dictum: "What is defeat? Nothing but education; nothing but the first steps to something better."

Thurlow Weed, who was a journalist for fifty-seven years, strong, sensible, genial, tactful, and of magnificent physique, who did so much to shape public policy in the Empire State, tells a most romantic story of his boyhood:--

"I cannot ascertain how much schooling I got at Catskill, probably less than a year, certainly not a year and a half, and this was when I was not more than five or six years old. I felt a necessity, at an early age, of trying to do something for my own support.

"My first employment was in sugar-making, an occupation to which I became much attached. I now look with great pleasure upon the days and nights passed in the sap-bush. The want of shoes (which, as the snow was deep, was no small privation) was the only drawback upon my happiness. I used, however, to tie pieces of an old rag carpet around my feet, and got along pretty well, chopping wood and gathering up sap. But when the spring advanced, and bare ground appeared in spots, I threw off the old carpet encumbrance and did my work barefoot.

"There is much leisure time for boys who are making maple sugar. I devoted this time to reading, when I could obtain books; but the farmers of that period had few or no books, save their Bibles. I borrowed books whenever and wherever I could.

"I heard that a neighbor, three miles off, had borrowed from a still more distant neighbor a book of great interest. I started off, barefoot, in the snow, to obtain the treasure. There were spots of bare ground, upon which I would stop to warm my feet. And there were also, along the road, occasional lengths of log-fence from which the snow had melted, and upon which it was a luxury to walk. The book was at home, and the good people consented, upon my promise that it should be neither torn nor soiled, to lend it to me. In returning with the prize, I was too happy to think of the snow or my naked feet.

"Candles were then among the luxuries, not the necessaries, of life. If boys, instead of going to bed after dark, wanted to read, they supplied themselves with pine knots, by the light of which, in a horizontal position, they pursued their studies. In this manner, with my body in the sugar-house, and my head out of doors, where the fat

pine was blazing, I read with intense interest the book I had borrowed, a 'History of the French Revolution.'"
Weed's next earning was in an iron foundry at Onondaga:

  "My business was, after a casting, to temper and prepare the mold-
ing 'dogs,' myself. This was night and day work. We ate salt pork and
rye and Indian bread, three times a day, and slept on straw in bunks.
I liked the excitement of a furnace life."

   When he went to the "Albany Argus" to learn the printing
business he worked from five in the morning till nine at night.

FROM HUMBLEST BEGINNINGS.

*The more difficulties one has to encounter,
within and without, the more significant
and the higher in inspiration his life will be.*

--Horace Bushnell.

   The story of Weed and of Greeley is not an uncommon
one in America. Some of the most eminent men on the globe have
struggled with poverty in early life and triumphed over it.
The astronomer Kepler, whose name can never die, was kept in
constant anxieties; and he told fortunes by astrology for a liveli-
hood, saying that astrology, as the daughter of astronomy, ought
to keep her mother. All sorts of service he had to accept; he made
almanacs and worked for any one who would pay him.
Linnaeus was so poor when getting his education that he had to
mend his shoes with folded paper, and often had to beg his meals
of his friends.
   During the ten years in which he made his greatest discover-
ies, Isaac Newton could hardly pay two shillings a week to the Royal
Society of which he was a member. Some of his friends wanted to

get him excused from this payment, but he would not allow them to act.

Humphry Davy had but a slender chance to acquire great scientific knowledge, yet he had true mettle in him, and he made even old pans, kettles, and bottles contribute to his success, as he experimented and studied in the attic of the apothecary store where he worked.

George Stephenson was one of eight children whose parents were so poor that all lived in a single room. George had to watch cows for a neighbor, but he managed to get time to make engines of clay, with hemlock sticks for pipes. At seventeen he had charge of an engine, with his father for fireman. He could neither read nor write, but the engine was his teacher, and he a faithful student. While the other hands were playing games or loafing in liquor shops during the holidays, George was taking his machine to pieces, cleaning it, studying it, and making experiments in engines. When he had become famous as a great inventor of improvements in engines, those who had loafed and played called him lucky.

It was by steadfastly keeping at it, by indomitable will power, that these men won their positions in life.

> "We rise by the things that are under our feet;
> By what we have mastered of good or gain."

TALENT IN TATTERS.

Among the companions of Sir Joshua Reynolds, while he was studying his art at Rome, was a fellow-pupil of the name of Astley. They made an excursion, with some others, on a sultry day, and all except Astley took off their coats. After several taunts he was persuaded to do the same, and displayed on the back of his waistcoat a foaming waterfall. Distress had compelled him to patch his clothes with one of his own landscapes.

James Sharpies, the celebrated blacksmith artist of England, was very poor, but he often rose at three o'clock to copy books he could not buy. He would walk eighteen miles to Manchester and back after a hard day's work, to buy a shilling's worth of artist's materials. He would ask for the heaviest work in the blacksmith shop, because it took a longer time to heat at the forge, and he could thus have many spare minutes to study the precious book, which he propped up against the chimney. He was a great miser of spare moments, and used every one as though he might never see another. He devoted his leisure hours for five years to that wonderful production, "The Forge," copies of which are to be seen in many a home. It was by one unwavering aim, carried out by an iron will, that he wrought out his life triumph.

"That boy will beat me one day," said an old painter as he watched a little fellow named Michael Angelo making drawings of pot and brushes, easel and stool, and other articles in the studio. The barefoot boy did persevere until he had overcome every difficulty and become the greatest master of art the world has known. Although Michael Angelo made himself immortal in three different occupations,--and his fame might well rest upon his dome of St. Peter as an architect, upon his "Moses" as a sculptor, or upon his "Last Judgment" as a painter,--yet we find by his correspondence, now in the British Museum, that when he was at work on his colossal bronze statue of Pope Julius II., he was so poor that he could not have his younger brother come to visit him at Bologna, because he had but one bed in which he and three of his assistants slept together. Yet

> *"The star of an unconquered will*
> *Arose in his breast,*
> *Serene, and resolute and still,*
> *And calm and self-possessed."*

CONCENTRATED ENERGY.

The struggles and triumphs of those who are bound to win is a never-ending tale. Nor will the procession of enthusiastic workers cease so long as the globe is turning on its axle.

Say what we will of genius, specialized in a hundred callings, yet the fact remains that no amount of genius has ever availed upon the earth unless enforced by will power to overcome the obstacles that hedge about every one who would rise above the circumstances in which he was born, or become greater than his calling. Was not Virgil the son of a porter, Horace of a shopkeeper, Demosthenes of a cutler, Milton of a money scrivener, Shakespeare of a wool stapler, and Cromwell of a brewer?

Ben Jonson, when following his trade of a mason, worked on Lincoln's Inn in London with trowel in hand and a book in his pocket. Joseph Hunter was a carpenter in youth, Robert Burns a plowman, Keats a druggist, Thomas Carlyle and Hugh Miller masons. Dante and Descartes were soldiers. Cardinal Wolsey, Defoe, and Kirke White were butchers' sons. Faraday was the son of a hostler, and his teacher, Humphry Davy, was an apprentice to an apothecary. Kepler was a waiter boy in a German hotel, Bunyan a tinker, Copernicus the son of a Polish baker. They rose by being greater than their callings, as Arkwright rose above mere barbering, Bunyan above tinkering, Wilson above shoemaking, Lincoln above rail-splitting, and Grant above tanning. By being first-class barbers, tinkers, shoemakers, rail-splitters, tanners, they acquired the power which enabled them to become great inventors, authors, statesmen, generals. John Kay, the inventor of the fly-shuttle, James Hargreaves, who introduced the spinning-jenny, and Samuel Compton, who originated mule-spinning, were all artisans, uneducated and poor, but were endowed with natural faculties which enabled them to make a more enduring impression upon the world than anything that could have been done by the mere power of scholarship or wealth.

It cannot be said of any of these great names that their individual courses in life would have been what they were, had there been lacking a superb will power resistless as the tide to bear them upward and onward.

"Let Fortune empty her whole quiver on me,
I have a soul that, like an ample shield,
Can take in all, and verge enough for more;
Fate was not mine, nor am I Fate's:
Souls know no conquerors."

--Dryden.

Chapter VI. Staying Power

"Never give up, there are chances and changes,
Helping the hopeful, a hundred to one;
And, through the chaos, High Wisdom arranges
Ever success, if you'll only hold on.
Never give up; for the wisest is boldest,
Knowing that Providence mingles the cup,
And of all maxims, the best, as the oldest,
Is the stern watchword of 'Never give up!'"
Be firm; one constant element of luck
Is genuine, solid, old Teutonic pluck.

--Holmes.

Success in most things depends on knowing
how long it takes to succeed

--Montesquieu.

THE power to hold on is characteristic of all men who have accomplished anything great; they may lack in some other particular, have many weaknesses or eccentricities, but the quality of persistence is never absent from a successful man. No matter what opposition he meets or what discouragement overtakes him, drudgery cannot disgust him, obstacles cannot discourage him, labor cannot weary him; misfortune, sorrow, and reverses cannot harm him. It is not so much brilliancy of intellect, or fertility of resource, as persistency of effort, constancy of purpose, that makes a great man. Those who succeed in life are the men and women who keep everlastingly at it, who do not believe themselves geniuses, but who know that if they ever accomplish anything they must do it by determined and persistent industry.

Audubon after years of forest life had two hundred of his priceless drawings destroyed by mice.

"A poignant flame," he relates, "pierced my brain like an arrow of fire, and for several weeks I was prostrated with fever. At length physical and moral strength awoke within me. Again I took my gun, my game-bag, my portfolio, and my pencils, and plunged once more into the depths of the forests."

All are familiar with the misfortune of Carlyle while writing his "History of the French Revolution." After the first volume was ready for the press, he loaned the manuscript to a neighbor, who left it lying on the floor, and the servant girl took it to kindle the fire. It was a bitter disappointment, but Carlyle was not the man to give up. After many months of poring Over hundreds of volumes of authorities and scores of manuscripts, he reproduced that which had burned in a few minutes.

PROCEED, AND LIGHT WILL DAWN.

The slightest acquaintance with literary history would bring to light a multitude of heroes of poverty or misfortune, of men and women perplexed and disheartened, who have yet aroused themselves to new effort at every new obstacle.

It is related by Arago that he found under the cover of a text book he was binding a short note from D'Alembert to a student:

"Go on, sir, go on. The difficulties you meet with will resolve themselves as you advance. Proceed; and light will dawn, and shine with
increasing clearness on your path."

"That maxim," said Arago, "was my greatest master in mathemat-
ics."

Had Balzac been easily discouraged he would have hesitated
at the words of warning given by his father:

"Do you know that in literature a man must be either a king or a
beggar?"

"Very well," was the reply, "_I will be a king_."

His parents left him to his fate in a garret. For ten years he
fought terrible battles with hardship and poverty, but won a great
victory at last. He won it after producing forty novels that did not
win.

Zola's early manhood witnessed a bitter struggle against
poverty and deprivation. Until twenty he was a spoiled child; but, on
his father's death, he and his mother began the battle of life in Paris.
Of his dark time, Zola himself says:

"Often I went hungry for so long, that it seemed as if I must die. I
scarcely tasted meat from one month's end to another, and for two
days I lived on three apples. Fire, even on the coldest nights, was an
undreamed-of luxury; and I was the happiest man in Paris when I
could get a candle, by the light of which I might study at night."
Samuel Johnson's bare feet at Oxford showed through the holes in
his shoes, yet he threw out at his window the new pair that some
one left at his door. He lived for a time in London on nine cents a
day. For thirteen years he had a hard struggle with want. John Locke
once lived on bread and water in a Dutch garret, and Heyne slept
many a night on a barn floor with only a book for his pillow. It was
to poverty as a thorn urging the breast of Harriet Martineau that
we owe her writings.

There are no more interesting pages in biography than those
which record how Emerson, as a child, was unable to read the sec-

ond volume of a certain book, because his widowed mother could not afford the amount (five cents) necessary to obtain it from the circulating library.

"Poor fellow!" said Emerson, as he looked at his delicately-reared little son, "how much he loses by not having to go through the hard experiences I had in my youth."

It was through the necessity laid upon him to earn that Emerson made his first great success in life as a teacher. "I know," he said, "no such unquestionable badge and ensign of a sovereign mind as that tenacity of purpose, which, through all change of companions or parties or fortunes, changes never, bates no jot of heart or hope, but wearies out opposition and arrives at its port."

"SHE CAN NEVER SUCCEED."

Louisa Alcott earned two hundred thousand dollars by her pen. Yet, when she was first dreaming of her power, her father handed her a manuscript one day that had been rejected by Mr. Fields, editor of the "Atlantic," with the message:

"Tell Louisa to stick to her teaching; she can never succeed as a writer."

"Tell him I *will* succeed as a writer, and some day I shall write for the 'Atlantic.'"

Not long after she wrote for the "Atlantic" a poem that Longfellow attributed to Emerson. And there came a time when she wrote in her diary:

"Twenty years ago I resolved to make the family independent if I could. At forty, that is done. Debts all paid, even the outlawed ones, and we have enough to be comfortable. It has cost me my health, perhaps."

"I TRAMPLE ON IMPOSSIBILITIES":

So it was said by Lord Chatham. "Why," asked Mirabeau, "should we call ourselves men, unless it be to succeed in everything everywhere?"

"It is all very well," said Charles J. Fox, "to tell me that a young man has distinguished himself by a brilliant first speech. He may go on satisfied with his first triumph; but show me a young man who has not succeeded at first, and has then gone on, and I will back that man to do better than those who succeeded at the first trial." Cobden broke down completely the first time he appeared on a platform in Manchester, and the chairman apologized for him; but he did not give up speaking until every poor man in England had a larger, better, and cheaper loaf. Young Disraeli sprung from a hated and persecuted race, pushed his way up through the middle classes and upper classes, until he stood self-poised upon the topmost round of political and social power. At first he was scoffed at, ridiculed, rebuffed, hissed from the House of Commons; he simply said, "The time will come when you will hear me." The time did come, and he swayed the sceptre of England for a quarter of a century.

How massive was the incalculable reserve power of Lincoln as a youth; or of President Garfield, wood-chopper, bell-ringer, and sweeper-general in college!

PERSISTENT PURPOSE.

We hear a great deal of talk about genius, talent, luck, chance, cleverness, and fine manners playing a large part in one's success. Leaving out luck and chance, all these elements are important factors. Yet the possession of any or all of them, unaccompanied by a definite aim, a determined purpose, will not insure success. Men drift into business. They drift into society. They drift into politics. They drift into what they fondly and but vainly imagine is religion. If winds and tides are favorable, all is well; if not, all is wrong. Stalker says: "Most men merely drift through life, and the work they do is determined by a hundred different circumstances; they might as well be doing anything else, or they would prefer to be doing nothing at all." Yet whatever else may have been lacking in the giants of the race, the men who have been conspicuously successful have all had one characteristic in common--doggedness and persistence of purpose.

It does not matter how clever a youth may be, whether he leads his class in college or outshines all the other boys in his community, he will never succeed if he lacks this essential of determined persistence. Many men who might have made brilliant musicians, artists, teachers, lawyers, able physicians or surgeons, in spite of predictions to the contrary, have fallen short of success because deficient in this quality.

Persistency of purpose is a power. It creates confidence in others. Everybody believes in the determined man. When he undertakes anything his battle is half won, because not only he himself, but every one who knows him, believes that he will accomplish whatever he sets out to do. People know that it is useless to oppose a man who uses his stumbling-blocks as stepping-stones; who is not afraid of defeat; who never, in spite of calumny or criticism, shrinks from his task; who never shirks responsibility; who always keeps his compass pointed to the north star of his purpose, no matter what storms may rage about him.

The persistent man never stops to consider whether he is succeeding or not. The only question with him is how to push ahead, to get a little farther along, a little nearer his goal. Whether it lead over mountains, rivers, or morasses, he must reach it. Every other consideration is sacrificed to this one dominant purpose. The success of a dull or average youth and the failure of a brilliant one is a constant surprise in American history. But if the different cases are closely analyzed we shall find that the explanation lies in the staying power of the seemingly dull boy, the ability to stand firm as a rock under all circumstances, to allow nothing to divert him from his purpose.

THREE NECESSARY THINGS.

"Three things are necessary," said Charles Sumner, "first, backbone; second, backbone; third, backbone."

A good chance alone is nothing. Education is nothing without strong and vigorous resolution and stamina to make one accomplish something in the world. An encouraging start is nothing without backbone. A man who cannot stand erect, who wabbles first one way and then the other, who has no opinion of his own, or courage to think his own thought, is of very little use in this world. It is grit, it is perseverance, it is moral stamina and courage that govern the world.

At the trial of the seven bishops of the Church of England for refusing to aid the king to overthrow the Protestant faith, it was necessary to watch the officers at the doors, lest they send food to some juryman, and aid him to starve the others into an agreement. Nothing was allowed to be sent in but water for the jurymen to wash in, and they were so thirsty they drank it up. At first nine were for acquitting, and three for convicting. Two of the minority soon gave way; the third, Arnold, was obstinate. He declined to argue. Austin said to him, "Look at me. I am the largest and the strongest of the twelve; and before I will find such a petition as this libel, here will I stay till I am no bigger than a tobacco pipe." Arnold yielded at six in the morning.

SUCCESS AGAINST ODDS.

"Yes, to this thought I hold with firm persistence;
The last result of wisdom stamps it true:
He only earns his freedom and existence
Who daily conquers them anew."

--Goethe.

"It is interesting to notice how some minds seem almost to create themselves," says Irving, "springing up under every disadvantage, and working their solitary but irresistible way through a thousand obstacles." Opposing circumstances create strength. Opposition gives us greater power of resistance. To overcome one barrier gives us greater ability to overcome the next. History is full of examples of men and women who have redeemed themselves from disgrace, poverty, and misfortune, by the firm resolution of an iron will.

Success is not measured by what a man accomplishes, but by the opposition he has encountered, and the courage with which he has maintained the struggle against overwhelming odds. Not the distance we have run, but the obstacles we have overcome, the disadvantages under which we have made the race, will decide the prizes.

"It is defeat," says Henry Ward Beecher, "that turns bone to flint, and gristle to muscle, and makes men invincible, and formed those heroic natures that are now in ascendency in the world. Do not, then, be afraid of defeat. You are never so near to victory as when defeated in a good cause."

Governor Seymour of New York, a man of great force and character, said, in reviewing his life: "If I were to wipe out twenty acts, what should they be? Should it be my business mistakes, my foolish acts (for I suppose all do foolish acts occasionally), my grievances? No; for, after all, these are the very things by which I have profited. So I finally concluded I should expunge, instead of my mistakes, my triumphs. I could not afford to dismiss the tonic of mortification, the refinement of sorrow; I needed them every one."

"Every condition, be it what it may," says Channing, "has hardships, hazards, pains. We try to escape them; we pine for a sheltered lot, for a smooth path, for cheering friends, and unbroken success. But Providence ordains storms, disasters, hostilities, sufferings; and the great question whether we shall live to any purpose or not, whether we shall grow strong in mind and heart, or be weak and pitiable, depends on nothing so much as on our use of the adverse circumstances. Outward evils are designed to school our passions, and to rouse our faculties and virtues into intenser action. Sometimes they seem to create new powers. Difficulty is the element, and resistance the true work of man. Self-culture never goes on so fast as when embarrassed circumstances, the opposition of men or the elements, unexpected changes of the times, or other forms of suffering, instead of disheartening, throw us on our inward resources, turn us for strength to God, clear up to us the great purpose of life, and inspire calm resolution. No greatness or goodness is worth much, unless tried in these fires."

> *"Better to stem with heart and hand*
> *The roaring tide of life, than lie,*
> *Unmindful, on its flowery strand,*
> *Of God's occasions drifting by!*
> *Better with naked nerve to bear*
> *The needles of this goading air,*
> *Than in the lap of sensual ease forego*
> *The godlike power to do, the godlike aim to know. "*

> --Whittier.

Chapter VII. The Degree of "O.O."

WHEN Moody first visited Ireland he was introduced by a friend to an Irish merchant who asked at once:

"Is he an O.O.?"

"Out and Out"--that was what "O.O." stood for.

"Out and Out" for God--that was what this merchant meant. He indeed is but a wooden man, and a poor stick at that, who is decided in everything else, but who never knows "where he is at" in all moral relations, being religiously nowhere.

The early books of the Hebrews have much to say about "The Valley of Decision" and the development of "Out and Out" moral character.

Wofully lacking in a well-balanced will power is the man who stands side by side with moral evil personified, in hands with it, to serve it willingly as a tool and servant.

Morally made in God's image, what is more sane, more wholesome, more fitting, for a man than his rising up promptly, decidedly, to make the Divine Will his own will in all moral action, to take it as the supreme guide to go by? It is the glory of the human will to coincide with the Divine Will. Doing this, a man's Iron Will, instead of being a malignant selfish power, will be useful in uplifting mankind.

God has spoken, or he has not spoken. If he has spoken, the

wise will hear.

> "We search the world for truth; we cull
> The good, the pure, the beautiful,
> From graven stone and written scroll,
> From all the flower-fields of the soul:
> And, weary seekers of the best,
> We come back laden from our quest,
> To find that all the sages said
> Is in the BOOK our mother read."
>
>   --Whittier.

> "O earth that blooms and birds that sing,
> O stars that shine when all is dark!
> In type and symbol thou dost bring
> The Life Divine, and bid us hark,
> That we may catch the chant sublime,
> And, rising, pass the bounds of time;
> So shall we win the goal divine,
> Our immortality."
>
>   --Carrol Norton.

The Two Babylons
Alexander Hislop

QTY

You may be surprised to learn that many traditions of Roman Catholicism in fact don't come from Christ's teachings but from an ancient Babylonian "Mystery" religion that was centered on Nimrod, his wife Semiramis, and a child Tammuz. This book shows how this ancient religion transformed itself as it incorporated Christ into its teachings...

Religion/History   Pages:353

ISBN: *1-59462-010-5*   MSRP *$22.95*

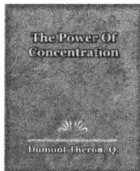

The Power Of Concentration
Theron Q. Dumont

It is of the utmost value to learn how to concentrate. To make the greatest success of anything you must be able to concentrate your entire thought upon the idea you are working on. The person that is able to concentrate utilizes all constructive thoughts and shuts out all destructive ones...

Self Help/Inspirational   Pages:196

ISBN: *1-59462-141-1*   MSRP *$14.95*

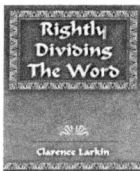

Rightly Dividing The Word
Clarence Larkin

The "Fundamental Doctrines" of the Christian Faith are clearly outlined in numerous books on Theology, but they are not available to the average reader and were mainly written for students. The Author has made it the work of his ministry to preach the "Fundamental Doctrines." To this end he has aimed to express them in the simplest and clearest manner...

Religion   Pages:352

ISBN: *1-59462-334-1*   MSRP *$23.45*

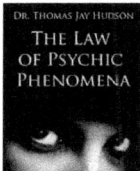

The Law of Psychic Phenomena
Thomson Jay Hudson

"I do not expect this book to stand upon its literary merits; for if it is unsound in principle, felicity of diction cannot save it, and if sound, homeliness of expression cannot destroy it. My primary object in offering it to the public is to assist in bringing Psychology within the domain of the exact sciences. That this has never been accomplished..."

New Age   Pages:420

ISBN: *1-59462-124-1*   MSRP *$29.95*

Beautiful Joe
Marshall Saunders

When Marshall visited the Moore family in 1892, she discovered Joe, a dog they had nursed back to health from his previous abusive home to live a happy life. So moved was she, that she wrote this classic masterpiece which won accolades and was recognized as a heartwarming symbol for humane animal treatment...

Fiction   Pages:256

ISBN: *1-59462-261-2*   MSRP *$18.45*

The Codes Of Hammurabi And Moses - W. W. Davies

The discovery of the Hammurabi Code is one of the greatest achievements of archaeology, and is of paramount interest, not only to the student of the Bible, but also to all those interested in ancient history...

Religion   Pages:132

ISBN: *1-59462-338-4*   MSRP *$12.95*

The Thirty-Six Dramatic Situations
Georges Polti

An incredibly useful guide for aspiring authors and playwrights. This volume categorizes every dramatic situation which could occur in a story and describes them in a list of 36 situations. A great aid to help inspire or formalize the creative writing process...

Self Help/Reference   Pages:204

ISBN: *1-59462-134-9*   MSRP *$15.95*

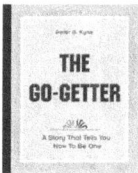

The Go-Getter
Kyne B. Peter

QTY

The Go Getter is the story of William Peck. He was a war veteran and amputee who will not be refused what he wants. Peck not only fights to find employment but continually proves himself more than competent at the many difficult test that are throw his way in the course of his early days with the Ricks Lumber Company...

Business/Self Help/Inspirational   Pages:68

ISBN: *1-59462-186-1*   MSRP *$8.95*

Self Mastery
Emile Coue

Emile Coue came up with novel way to improve the lives of people. He was a pharmacist by trade and often saw ailing people. This lead him to develop autosuggestion, a form of self-hypnosis. At the time his theories weren't popular but over the years evidence is mounting that he was indeed right all along...

New Age/Self Help   Pages:98

ISBN: *1-59462-189-6*   MSRP *$7.95*

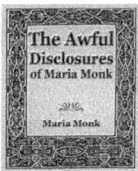

The Awful Disclosures Of
Maria Monk

"I cannot banish the scenes and characters of this book from my memory. To me it can never appear like an amusing fable, or lose its interest and importance. The story is one which is continually before me, and must return fresh to my mind with painful emotions as long as I live..."

Religion   Pages:232

ISBN: *1-59462-160-8*   MSRP *$17.95*

As a Man Thinketh
James Allen

"This little volume (the result of meditation and experience) is not intended as an exhaustive treatise on the much-written-upon subject of the power of thought. It is suggestive rather than explanatory, its object being to stimulate men and women to the discovery and perception of the truth that by virtue of the thoughts which they choose and encourage..."

Inspirational/Self Help   Pages:80

ISBN: *1-59462-231-0*   MSRP *$9.45*

The Enchanted April
Elizabeth Von Arnim

It began in a woman's club in London on a February afternoon, an uncomfortable club, and a miserable afternoon when Mrs. Wilkins, who had come down from Hampstead to shop and had lunched at her club, took up The Times from the table in the smoking-room...

Fiction   Pages:368

ISBN: *1-59462-150-0*   MSRP *$23.45*

Holland - The History Of Netherlands
Thomas Colley Grattan

Thomas Grattan was a prestigious writer from Dublin who served as British Consul to the US. Among his works is an authoritative look at the history of Holland. A colorful and interesting look at history....

History/Politics   Pages:408

ISBN: *1-59462-137-3*   MSRP *$26.95*

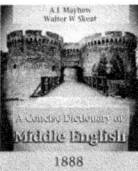

A Concise Dictionary of Middle English
A. L. Mayhew
Walter W. Skeat

The present work is intended to meet, in some measure, the requirements of those who wish to make some study of Middle-English, and who find a difficulty in obtaining such assistance as will enable them to find out the meanings and etymologies of the words most essential to their purpose...

Reference/History   Pages:332

ISBN: *1-59462-119-5*   MSRP *$29.95*

www.bookjungle.com *email: sales@bookjungle.com fax: 630-214-0564 mail: Book Jungle PO Box 2226 Champaign, IL 61825*

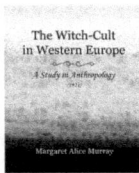

The Witch-Cult in Western Europe
Margaret Murray
The mass of existing material on this subject is so great that I have not attempted to make a survey of the whole of European "Witchcraft" but have confined myself to an intensive study of the cult in Great Britain. In order, however, to obtain a clearer understanding of the ritual and beliefs I have had recourse to French and Flemish sources...

Occult   Pages:308
ISBN: *1-59462-126-8*   MSRP *$22.45*

QTY

The Science Of Psychic Healing
Yogi Ramacharaka
This book is not a book of theories it deals with facts. Its author regards the best of theories as but working hypotheses to be used only until better ones present themselves. The "fact" is the principal thing the essential thing to uncover which the tool, theory, is used...

New Age/Health   Pages:180
ISBN: *1-59462-140-3*   MSRP *$13.95*

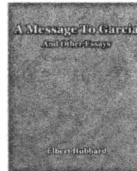

Bible Myths
Thomas Doane
In pursuing the study of the Bible Myths, facts pertaining thereto, in a condensed form, seemed to be greatly needed, and nowhere to be found. Widely scattered through hundreds of ancient and modern volumes, most of the contents of this book may indeed be found; but any previous attempt to trace exclusively the myths and legends...

Religion/History   Pages:644
ISBN: *1-59462-163-2*   MSRP *$38.95*

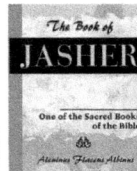

Tertium Organum
P. D. Ouspensky
A truly mind expanding writing that combines science with mysticism with unprecedented elegance. He presents the world we live in as a multi dimensional world and time as a motion through this world. But this isn't a cold and purely analytical explanation but a masterful presentation filled with similes and analogies...

New Age   Pages:356
ISBN: *1-59462-205-1*   MSRP *$23.95*

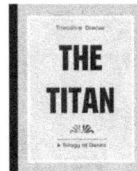

Advance Course in Yogi Philosophy
Yogi Ramacharaka
"The twelve lessons forming this volume were originally issued in the shape of monthly lessons, known as "The Advanced Course in Yogi Philosophy and Oriental Occultism" during a period of twelve months beginning with October, 1904, and ending September, 1905."

Philosophy/Inspirational/Self Help Pages:340
ISBN: *1-59462-229-9*   MSRP *$22.95*

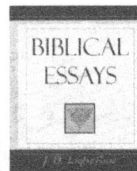

Ambassador Morgenthau's Story
Henry Morgenthau
"By this time the American people have probably become convinced that the Germans deliberately planned the conquest of the world. Yet they hesitate to convict on circumstantial evidence and for this reason all eye witnesses to this, the greatest crime in modern history, should volunteer their testimony..."

History   Pages:472
ISBN: *1-59462-244-2*   MSRP *$29.95*

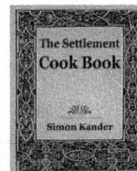

The Aquarian Gospel of Jesus the Christ
Levi Dowling
A retelling of Jesus' story which tells us what happened during the twenty year gap left by the Bible's New Testament. It tells of his travels to the far-east where he studied with the masters and fought against the rigid caste system. This book has enjoyed a resurgence in modern America and provides spiritual insight with charm. Its influences can be seen throughout the Age of Aquarius.

Religion   Pages:264
ISBN: *1-59462-321-X*   MSRP *$18.95*

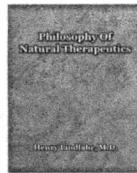

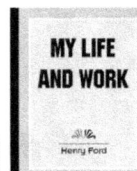

Philosophy Of Natural Therapeutics
Henry Lindlahr
We invite the earnest cooperation in this great work of all those who have awakened to the necessity for more rational living and for radical reform in healing methods...

Health/Philosophy/Self Help   Pages:552
ISBN: *1-59462-132-2*   MSRP *$34.95*

QTY

A Message to Garcia
Elbert Hubbard
This literary trifle, A Message to Garcia, was written one evening after supper, in a single hour. It was on the Twenty-second of February, Eighteen Hundred Ninety-nine, Washington's Birthday, and we were just going to press with the March Philistine...

New Age/Fiction   Pages:92
ISBN: *1-59462-144-6*   MSRP *$9.95*

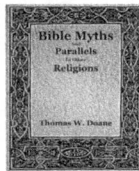

The Book of Jasher
Alcuinus Flaccus Albinus
The Book of Jasher is an historical religious volume that many consider as a missing holy book from the Old Testament. Particularly studied by the Church of Later Day Saints and historians, it covers the history of the world from creation until the period of Judges in Israel. It's authenticity is bolstered due to a reference to the Book of Jasher in the Bible in Joshua 10:13

Religion/History   Pages:276
ISBN: *1-59462-197-7*   MSRP *$18.95*

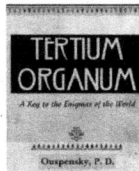

The Titan
Theodore Dreiser
"When Frank Algernon Cowperwood emerged from the Eastern District Penitentiary, in Philadelphia he realized that the old life he had lived in that city since boyhood was ended. His youth was gone, and with it had been lost the great business prospects of his earlier manhood. He must begin again..."

Fiction   Pages:564
ISBN: *1-59462-220-5*   MSRP *$33.95*

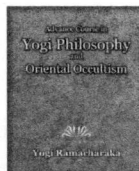

Biblical Essays
J. B. Lightfoot
About one-third of the present volume has already seen the light. The opening essay "On the Internal Evidence for the Authenticity and Genuineness of St John's Gospel" was published in the "Expositor" in the early months of 1890, and has been reprinted since...

Religion/History   Pages:480
ISBN: *1-59462-238-8*   MSRP *$30.95*

The Settlement Cook Book
Simon Kander
A legacy from the civil war, this book is a classic "American charity cookbook," which was used for fundraisers starting in Milwaukee. While it has transformed over the years, this printing provides great recipes from American history. Over two million copies have been sold. This volume contains a rich collection of recipes from noted chefs and hostesses of the turn of the century...

How-to   Pages:472
ISBN: *1-59462-256-6*   MSRP *$29.95*

My Life and Work
Henry Ford
Henry Ford revolutionized the world with his implementation of mass production for the Model T automobile.   Gain valuable business insight into his life and work with his own auto-biography... "We have only started on our development of our country we have not as yet, with all our talk of wonderful progress, done more than scratch the surface. The progress has been wonderful enough but..."

Biographies/History/Business   Pages:300
ISBN: *1-59462-198-5*   MSRP *$21.95*

QTY

The Rosicrucian Cosmo-Conception Mystic Christianity by *Max Heindel*   ISBN: *1-59462-188-8*   **$38.95**
The Rosicrucian Cosmo-conception is not dogmatic, neither does it appeal to any other authority than the reason of the student. It is: not controversial, but is: sent forth in the, hope that it may help to clear...   New Age/Religion Pages 646

Abandonment To Divine Providence by *Jean-Pierre de Caussade*   ISBN: *1-59462-228-0*   **$25.95**
"The Rev. Jean Pierre de Caussade was one of the most remarkable spiritual writers of the Society of Jesus in France in the 18th Century. His death took place at Toulouse in 1751. His works have gone through many editions and have been republished...   Inspirational/Religion Pages 400

Mental Chemistry by *Charles Haanel*   ISBN: *1-59462-192-6*   **$23.95**
Mental Chemistry allows the change of material conditions by combining and appropriately utilizing the power of the mind. Much like applied chemistry creates something new and unique out of careful combinations of chemicals the mastery of mental chemistry...   New Age Pages 354

The Letters of Robert Browning and Elizabeth Barret Barrett 1845-1846 vol II   ISBN: *1-59462-193-4*   **$35.95**
by *Robert Browning* and *Elizabeth Barrett*
Biographies Pages 596

Gleanings In Genesis (volume I) by *Arthur W. Pink*   ISBN: *1-59462-130-6*   **$27.45**
Appropriately has Genesis been termed "the seed plot of the Bible" for in it we have, in germ form, almost all of the great doctrines which are afterwards fully developed in the books of Scripture which follow...   Religion/Inspirational Pages 420

The Master Key by *L. W. de Laurence*   ISBN: *1-59462-001-6*   **$30.95**
In no branch of human knowledge has there been a more lively increase of the spirit of research during the past few years than in the study of Psychology, Concentration and Mental Discipline. The requests for authentic lessons in Thought Control, Mental Discipline and...   New Age/Business Pages 422

The Lesser Key Of Solomon Goetia by *L. W. de Laurence*   ISBN: *1-59462-092-X*   **$9.95**
This translation of the first book of the "Lemegton" which is now for the first time made accessible to students of Talismanic Magic was done, after careful collation and edition, from numerous Ancient Manuscripts in Hebrew, Latin, and French...   New Age/Occult Pages 92

Rubaiyat Of Omar Khayyam by *Edward Fitzgerald*   ISBN: *1-59462-332-5*   **$13.95**
Edward Fitzgerald, whom the world has already learned, in spite of his own efforts to remain within the shadow of anonymity, to look upon as one of the rarest poets of the century, was born at Bredfield, in Suffolk, on the 31st of March, 1809. He was the third son of John Purcell...   Music Pages 172

Ancient Law by *Henry Maine*   ISBN: *1-59462-128-4*   **$29.95**
The chief object of the following pages is to indicate some of the earliest ideas of mankind, as they are reflected in Ancient Law, and to point out the relation of those ideas to modern thought.   Religion/History Pages 452

Far-Away Stories by *William J. Locke*   ISBN: *1-59462-129-2*   **$19.45**
"Good wine needs no bush, but a collection of mixed vintage. does. And this book is just such a collection. Some of the stories I do not want to remain buried for ever in the museum files of dead magazine-numbers an author's not unpardonable vanity..."   Fiction Pages 272

Life of David Crockett by *David Crockett*   ISBN: *1-59462-250-7*   **$27.45**
'Colonel David Crockett was one of the most remarkable men of the times in which he lived. Born in humble life, but gifted with a strong will, an indomitable courage, and unremitting perseverance...   Biographies/New Age Pages 424

Lip-Reading by *Edward Nitchie*   ISBN: *1-59462-206-X*   **$25.95**
Edward B. Nitchie, founder of the New York School for the Hard of Hearing, now the Nitchie School of Lip-Reading, Inc, wrote "LIP-READING Principles and Practice". The development and perfecting of this meritorious work on lip-reading was an undertaking...   How-to Pages 400

A Handbook of Suggestive Therapeutics, Applied Hypnotism, Psychic Science   ISBN: *1-59462-214-0*   **$24.95**
by *Henry Munro*
Health/New Age/Health/Self-help Pages 376

A Doll's House: and Two Other Plays by *Henrik Ibsen*   ISBN: *1-59462-112-8*   **$19.95**
Henrik Ibsen created this classic when in revolutionary 1848 Rome. Introducing some striking concepts in playwriting for the realist genre, this play has been studied the world over.   Fiction/Classics/Plays 308

The Light of Asia by *sir Edwin Arnold*   ISBN: *1-59462-204-3*   **$13.95**
In this poetic masterpiece, Edwin Arnold describes the life and teachings of Buddha. The man who was to become known as Buddha to the world was born as Prince Gautama of India but he rejected the worldly riches and abandoned the reigns of power when...   Religion/History/Biographies Pages 170

The Complete Works of Guy de Maupassant by *Guy de Maupassant*   ISBN: *1-59462-157-8*   **$16.95**
"For days and days, nights and nights, I had dreamed of that first kiss which was to consecrate our engagement, and I knew not on what spot I should put my lips..."   Fiction/Classics Pages 240

The Art of Cross-Examination by *Francis L. Wellman*   ISBN: *1-59462-309-0*   **$26.95**
Written by a renowned trial lawyer, Wellman imparts his experience and uses case studies to explain how to use psychology to extract desired information through questioning.   How-to/Science/Reference Pages 408

Answered or Unanswered? by *Louisa Vaughan*   ISBN: *1-59462-248-5*   **$10.95**
Miracles of Faith in China   Religion Pages 112

The Edinburgh Lectures on Mental Science (1909) by *Thomas*   ISBN: *1-59462-008-3*   **$11.95**
This book contains the substance of a course of lectures recently given by the writer in the Queen Street Hail, Edinburgh. Its purpose is to indicate the Natural Principles governing the relation between Mental Action and Material Conditions...   New Age/Psychology Pages 148

Ayesha by *H. Rider Haggard*   ISBN: *1-59462-301-5*   **$24.95**
Verily and indeed it is the unexpected that happens! Probably if there was one person upon the earth from whom the Editor of this, and of a certain previous history, did not expect to hear again...   Classics Pages 380

Ayala's Angel by *Anthony Trollope*   ISBN: *1-59462-352-X*   **$29.95**
The two girls were both pretty, but Lucy who was twenty-one was supposed to be simple and comparatively unattractive, whereas Ayala was credited, as her Bombwhat romantic name might show, with poetic charm and a taste for romance. Ayala when her father died was nineteen...   Fiction Pages 484

The American Commonwealth by *James Bryce*   ISBN: *1-59462-286-8*   **$34.45**
An interpretation of American democratic political theory. It examines political mechanics and society from the perspective of Scotsman James Bryce   Politics Pages 572

Stories of the Pilgrims by *Margaret P. Pumphrey*   ISBN: *1-59462-116-0*   **$17.95**
This book explores pilgrims religious oppression in England as well as their escape to Holland and eventual crossing to America on the Mayflower, and their early days in New England...   History Pages 268

www.bookjungle.com *email: sales@bookjungle.com fax: 630-214-0564 mail: Book Jungle PO Box 2226 Champaign, IL 61825*

QTY

The Fasting Cure *by Sinclair Upton* ISBN: *1-59462-222-1* **$13.95**
In the Cosmopolitan Magazine for May, 1910, and in the Contemporary Review (London) for April, 1910, I published an article dealing with my experiences in fasting. I have written a great many magazine articles, but never one which attracted so much attention... New Age/Self Help/Health Pages 164

Hebrew Astrology *by Sepharial* ISBN: *1-59462-308-2* **$13.45**
In these days of advanced thinking it is a matter of common observation that we have left many of the old landmarks behind and that we are now pressing forward to greater heights and to a wider horizon than that which represented the mind-content of our progenitors... Astrology Pages 144

Thought Vibration or The Law of Attraction in the Thought World ISBN: *1-59462-127-6* **$12.95**
by William Walker Atkinson *Psychology/Religion Pages 144*

Optimism *by Helen Keller* ISBN: *1-59462-108-X* **$15.95**
Helen Keller was blind, deaf, and mute since 19 months old, yet famously learned how to overcome these handicaps, communicate with the world, and spread her lectures promoting optimism. An inspiring read for everyone... Biographies/Inspirational Pages 84

Sara Crewe *by Frances Burnett* ISBN: *1-59462-360-0* **$9.45**
In the first place, Miss Minchin lived in London. Her home was a large, dull, tall one, in a large, dull square, where all the houses were alike, and all the sparrows were alike, and where all the door-knockers made the same heavy sound... Childrens/Classic Pages 88

The Autobiography of Benjamin Franklin *by Benjamin Franklin* ISBN: *1-59462-135-7* **$24.95**
The Autobiography of Benjamin Franklin has probably been more extensively read than any other American historical work, and no other book of its kind has had such ups and downs of fortune. Franklin lived for many years in England, where he was agent... Biographies/History Pages 332

Name	
Email	
Telephone	
Address	
City, State ZIP	

☐ **Credit Card**   ☐ **Check / Money Order**

Credit Card Number	
Expiration Date	
Signature	

Please Mail to: Book Jungle
PO Box 2226
Champaign, IL 61825
or Fax to: 630-214-0564

ORDERING INFORMATION
web: *www.bookjungle.com*
email: *sales@bookjungle.com*
fax: *630-214-0564*
mail: *Book Jungle PO Box 2226 Champaign, IL 61825*
or PayPal *to sales@bookjungle.com*

Please contact us for bulk discounts

DIRECT-ORDER TERMS

**20% Discount if You Order
Two or More Books**
Free Domestic Shipping!
Accepted: Master Card, Visa,
Discover, American Express

www.ingramcontent.com/pod-product-compliance
Lightning Source LLC
LaVergne TN
LVHW081326060426
835511LV00011B/1878